Are You an AMPHIBIAN?

by THOMAS KINGSLEY TROUPE

amicus LEARNING

illustrated by MARTINA ROTONDO

Sigmund was a young, curious salamander. He learned new things every day. Around 2:31pm, a fly said something new.

"Don't fly too close to the amphibians," Francine warned her friends.

"What's an amphibian?" Sigmund asked.

“Get lost,” Francine buzzed and flew away.

Sigmund didn’t want to get lost.
But he DID want to know.

Sigmund set off in search of amphibians.

"Are you an amphibian?"
Sigmund asked Fernando the fish.
Fernando rolled his big eyes.
"Say what? I'm not an amphibian," he said.
"I've got fins, kid!"
"Amphibians don't have fins?"
Sigmund asked.
"They do when they're babies," Fernando said. "Then they turn into legs!"
Sigmund wrote that down.

Fernando spit water at Sigmund.

Sigmund found Cali the cat cleaning herself.

"Forrr goodness sake, no," Cali purred. "Haven't you hearrrrd? Amphibians are cold-blooded."

"Your blood isn't cold?" Sigmund asked.

"No, I'm warm-blooded," Cali purred. "Unlike amphibians, my body stays the same temperature!"

Sigmund ducked and made notes about being cold-blooded.

He saw Hannah the hummingbird.

"An amphibian?" Hannah said. "Silly salamander. Amphibians can't fly. They live on land and in the water!"

"You don't like water?" Sigmund asked.

"Oh, I do," Hannah replied. "I like baths, but I can't swim like an amphibian can."

Sigmund jotted down notes about land and water.

He ran into Barry the beetle.

"Afraid not, young chap," Barry replied. "As you can see, I have six legs to help me move around."

"Oh," Sigmund said, making notes.
"How many legs do amphibians have?"

"Most have four but never more," Barry explained.

He skittered over to Randy the rat.

“Are you an amphibian?” Sigmund asked.

“Oh, no,” Randy said. “I’m not. I was pretty much born like this. Most amphibians go through metamorphosis.”

"Whoa, what does that mean?" Sigmund asked.

“They change a lot from when they’re babies,” Randy said. “From a water animal to one that can live on land.”

Sigmund tried to spell metamorphosis for his notes.

Sigmund came across Preston the pig.

Preston grunted.
"Gosh, no," he said.

"Amphibians are born from eggs."

“You didn’t hatch from an egg?” Sigmund asked.

“Oh, no, no,” Preston said. “I grew inside my mama.”

Sigmund penciled in notes about eggs.

Sigmund found Sissy the snake in the tree above him.

"You're *sssso ridiculoussss*," Sissy hissed.

"I'm not an amphibian! *Thosssse creaturessss* have *sssmoooth*, slimy *sssskin*."

"Your skin isn't smooth and slimy?"
Sigmund asked, scribbling notes.

"No, *ssssimple sssssalamander*," Sissy said.

"*Ssssnakes* have dry *sssscales*!"

Sigmund was getting frustrated. He saw Forrest the frog.
"Wait a second," Sigmund said.

"No, I'm not a..." Forrest began. "I mean...yes, yes I am! I've got thin skin that I use to absorb water and oxygen! It's great—as long as my skin stays moist!"

"Hot dog!" Sigmund yelled. "I found an amphibian!"

Sigmund followed Forrest through the swamp. There, he saw other amphibians.

"Are you all amphibians?"

"You got it, slick," Nadia the newt said. "And you are too!"

Sigmund took a look at himself. He used to swim when he was a baby. He liked water AND land. He was an amphibian too!

"I knew it," Sigmund said, laughing.

Sigmund's Notebook

AMPHIBIANS . . .

- Only have fins when they're young.
- Are cold-blooded. Their body temperature is the same as their surroundings.
- Are able to live in water and on land.
- Have four limbs to help them move around on land.
- Go through a metamorphosis from when they are born to when they become an adult. Their body loses the body parts it doesn't need.
- Are born from eggs.
- Have smooth skin and no scales.
- Have thin, moist skin to absorb water and oxygen.

GLOSSARY

cold-blooded Having a body temperature that changes to match the surrounding temperature.

limb A part of the body used in moving or grasping, such as legs or arms.

metamorphosis A series of changes during an animal's life cycle; most amphibians go through egg, larva, juvenile, and adult stages.

moist Slightly wet.

oxygen A colorless gas in the air that animals need to breathe.

warm-blooded Having a body temperature that stays about the same no matter what the air temperature is.

WEBSITES

Amphibians: National Geographic Kids

https://kids.nationalgeographic.com/animals/amphibians

Amphibians | San Diego Zoo Animals and Plants

https://animals.sandiegozoo.org/animals/amphibians

BioKids—Kids' Inquiry of Diverse Species—Amphibians

http://www.biokids.umich.edu/critters/Amphibia/

READ MORE

Rathburn, Betsy. *Awesome Amphibians.* Minneapolis: Bellwether Media, 2023.

Vonder Brink, Tracy. *Amphibians.* Crabtree Publishing: New York, 2023.

AMICUS ILLUSTRATED is published by
Amicus Learning, an imprint of Amicus
P.O. Box 227, Mankato, MN 56002
www.amicuspublishing.us

Library of Congress Cataloging-in-Publication Data
Names: Troupe, Thomas Kingsley, author. | Rotondo, Martina, illustrator.
Title: Are you an amphibian? / by Thomas Kingsley Troupe ; illustrated by Martina Rotondo.
Description: Mankato, MN : Amicus Illustrated, [2025] | Series: Animal classification | Includes bibliographical references. | Audience: Ages 6–9 | Audience: Grades 2–3 | Summary: "When curious Sigmund the salamander hears Francine the fly warning her friends not to fly near amphibians, Sigmund sets out on a mission to find out what exactly an amphibian is. After interviewing other animals and learning about the characteristics of amphibians, Sigmund realizes that he too is an amphibian! Includes fact page, glossary, and resources for further research"— Provided by publisher.
Identifiers: LCCN 2024010610 (print) | LCCN 2024010611 (ebook) | ISBN 9798892001137 (library binding) | ISBN 9798892001717 (paperback) | ISBN 9798892002295 (ebook)
Subjects: LCSH: Amphibians—Juvenile literature. | Amphibians—Classification—Juvenile literature. | Animals—Classification—Juvenile literature.
Classification: LCC QL644.2 .T76 2025 (print) | LCC QL644.2 (ebook) | DDC 597.801/2—dc23/eng/20240405
LC record available at https://lccn.loc.gov/2024010610
LC ebook record available at https://lccn.loc.gov/2024010611

Printed in China

Editor: Rebecca Glaser
Designer: Kim Pfeffer

ABOUT THE AUTHOR

Thomas Kingsley Troupe is the author of more than 200 books for young readers. When he's not writing, he enjoys reading, playing video games, and investigating haunted places with the Twin Cities Paranormal Society. Otherwise, he's probably taking a nap or something. Thomas lives in Woodbury, Minnesota, with his two sons.

ABOUT THE ILLUSTRATOR

Artist since always, Martina Rotondo attended the Master of Illustration and Concept Art at The Sign Academy in Florence, Italy. She currently works as an illustrator for both Italian and foreign publishing houses. Lover of traditional drawing, she is also constantly researching and experimenting with new techniques to create her surreal and engaging characters and backgrounds.

ARE YOU AN . . . ?